JANE AUSTEN

A Treasure Trove

JANE AUSTEN: A TREASURE TROVE

Text by Debbi Marco

An Hachette UK Company
www.hachette.co.uk

Summersdale Publishers
Part of Octopus Publishing Group Limited
Carmelite House
50 Victoria Embankment
LONDON
EC4Y 0DZ
UK

www.summersdale.com

This FSC® label means
that materials used for
the product have been
responsibly sourced

MIX
Paper | Supporting
responsible forestry
FSC® C016973

The authorized representative in the EEA is Hachette Ireland, 8 Castlecourt Centre, Dublin 15, D15 XTP3, Ireland (email: info@hbgi.ie)

Printed and bound in Malaysia

ISBN: 978-1-83799-645-2

Substantial discounts on bulk quantities of Summersdale books are available to corporations, professional associations and other organizations. For details contact general enquiries: telephone: +44 (0) 1243 771107 or email: enquiries@summersdale.com.

JANE AUSTEN

A Treasure Trove

CONSTANCE MOORE

summersdale

CONTENTS

INTRODUCTION

At first glance, Jane Austen may appear as simply a writer of romantic fiction, but the truth is she was so much more. As a feminist who shunned societal expectations, she captured the Regency Era through her unique lens using quick wit and her sharp eye for observation. Her writing was also influenced by the Napoleonic wars, aided by the fact that both her brothers served in the military as admirals.

With her interests, it's not hard to imagine Austen fitting in with her modern-day peers on TikTok. Indeed, if she had been alive today, chances are she'd have been a top influencer with her forward-thinking ideas around feminism, gender roles and education.

In these pages we celebrate her humour and thoughts on love, marriage, money and society that she expressed either through her private correspondence or via characters in her novels with fun facts, trivia and quotes.

LOVE AND COURTSHIP

"My heart is, and always will be, yours."

Edward Ferrars to Elinor Dashwood,
Sense and Sensibility

FACT

During the Regency Era, through which Jane Austen lived, there were many rules surrounding courtship and the path to finding true love. Couples were very strictly policed by polite society and to fall foul of these rules would threaten their reputations and jeopardize their chances of an advantageous marriage. For example, a couple could not use each other's first names or get to know each other without their families' approval; if they danced more than two sets together society would expect them to be betrothed and they had to be chaperoned at all times to protect their virtue.

"In vain I have struggled. It will not do. My feelings will not be repressed. You must allow me to tell you how ardently I admire and love you."

Mr Darcy to Elizabeth Bennet, Pride and Prejudice

"... the more I know of the world, the more am I convinced that I shall never see a man whom I can really love. I require so much!"

Marianne Dashwood to her mother, Sense and Sensibility

To you I shall say, as I have often said before, do not be in a hurry, the right man will come at last...

Letter to Fanny Knight, her niece

"A lady's imagination is very rapid; it jumps from admiration to love, from love to matrimony in a moment."

Mr Darcy to Caroline Bingley, Pride and Prejudice

"If I loved you less, I might be able to talk about it more."

Mr Knightley to Emma Woodhouse, Emma

"Poor fellow! He is much distracted by jealousy, which I am not sorry for, as I know no better support of love."

Lady Susan to Mrs Johnson, Lady Susan

... no young lady can be justified in falling in love before the gentleman's love is declared, it must be very improper that a young lady should dream of a gentleman before the gentleman is first known to have dreamt of her.

Northanger Abbey

"I pay very little regard," said Mrs Grant, "to what any young person says on the subject of marriage. If they profess a disinclination for it, I only set it down that they have not yet seen the right person."

Mrs Grant, Mansfield Park

TRIVIA

While couples might court each other for up to four years before getting married, often taking chaperoned walks together or having tea with each other's families, what was the average age to get married during the Regency Era?

a) Twenties

b) Thirties

c) Teens

Most of what we know about Jane Austen comes from letters to her sister, Cassandra. It is believed she wrote about 3,000 but Cassandra burned many of them because Jane was too forthright about neighbours, family members and illness. How many letters survived?

a) 16

b) 160

c) 1,600

... there could have been no two hearts so open, no tastes so similar, no feelings so in unison, no countenances so beloved.

Persuasion

"Where the heart is really attached, I know very well how little one can be pleased with the attention of anybody else."

Isabella Thorpe to Catherine Morland,
Northanger Abbey

"As for Willoughby – to say that I shall soon or that I shall ever forget him, would be idle. His remembrance can be overcome by no change of circumstances or opinions. But it shall be regulated, it shall he checked by religion, by reason, by constant employment."

Marianne Dashwood to Elinor Dashwood,
Sense and Sensibility

FACT

Despite remaining steadfastly single all her life, Jane Austen actually fell deeply in love when she was just 20 years old. The man in question was an Irishman called Tom Lefroy. However, regardless of the depth of their feelings for each other, his family wanted him to marry a wealthier woman and so their relationship never progressed. It's no wonder that dowries and marrying for material wealth were key themes in many of her novels.

"In nine cases out of ten a woman had better show more affection than she feels."

Charlotte Lucas to Elizabeth Bennet,
Pride and Prejudice

———————∞○○○∞———————

Mr Knightley could not impute to Emma a more relenting heart than she possessed, or a heart more disposed to accept of his.

Emma

When he was present she had no eyes for anyone else. Everything he did, was right. Everything he said, was clever. If their evenings at the park were concluded with cards, he cheated himself and all the rest of the party to get her a good hand. If dancing formed the amusement of the night, they were partners for half the time; and when obliged to separate for a couple of dances, were careful to stand together, and scarcely spoke a word to anybody else. Such conduct made them of course most exceedingly laughed at; but ridicule could not shame, and seemed hardly to provoke them.

Sense and Sensibility

MEN AND WOMEN

"Heaven forbid! That would be the greatest misfortune of all! To find a man agreeable whom one is determined to hate! Do not wish me such an evil."

Elizabeth Bennet to Charlotte Lucas,
Pride and Prejudice

FACT

Jane was one of the first writers to capture "the female gaze" in her writing, a theme explored by journalist Megan Garber. For example, in *Pride and Prejudice*, Elizabeth Bennet is the "subject" and Mr Darcy is the "object" of Elizabeth's gaze. For a long time the inner thoughts and observations of women had never been considered, but Jane changed all this with her wit and charm.

"But I hate to hear you talking so like a fine gentleman, and as if women were all fine ladies, instead of rational creatures. We none of us expect to be in smooth waters all our days."

Mrs Croft to Captain Wentworth, Persuasion

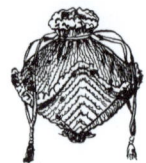

"A man would always wish to give a woman a better home than the one he takes her from; and he who can do it, where there is no doubt of her regard, must, I think, be the happiest of mortals."

Mr Knightley to Emma Woodhouse, Emma

"There is no charm equal to tenderness of heart," said she afterwards to herself. "There is nothing to be compared to it. Warmth and tenderness of heart, with an affectionate, open manner, will beat all the clearness of head in the world, for attraction, I am sure it will. It is tenderness of heart which makes my dear father so generally beloved – which gives Isabella all her popularity. I have it not – but I know how to prize and respect it."

Emma Woodhouse, *Emma*

"If there is anything disagreeable going on men are always sure to get out of it..."

Mary Musgrove, Persuasion

———∞OOO∞———

"... I think very highly of the understanding of all the women in the world – especially of those – whoever they may be – with whom I happen to be in company."

Henry Tilney to Catherine Morland,
Northanger Abbey

———∞OOO∞———

Dare not say that man forgets sooner than woman, that his love has an earlier death.

Captain Wentworth's letter to Anne Elliot, Persuasion

"No man is offended by another man's admiration of the woman he loves; it is the woman only who can make it a torment."

Henry Tilney to Catherine Morland,
Northanger Abbey

━━━━━━━━━━◦○Ο○◦━━━━━━━━━━

"What are young men to rocks and mountains?"

Elizabeth Bennet, Pride and Prejudice

TRIVIA

Women had very few rights to begin with in the Regency Era but once they married, they lost even more of their rights because they were viewed as the legal property of their husbands. What would a woman lose control of once married?

a) Custody of her children if divorced

b) Her property and finances

c) All of the above

Jane was born in December 1775, but not baptized until several months later. Why?

a) Her parents forgot

b) Her father had to pay off his debts to be allowed to have his daughter baptized

c) It was a very harsh winter so they were unable to get to the church

"He is also handsome," replied Elizabeth, "which a young man ought likewise to be, if he possibly can. His character is thereby complete."

Elizabeth Bennet to Jane Bennet, Pride and Prejudice

"... when a young man, be who he will, comes and makes love to a pretty girl, and promises marriage, he has no business to fly off from his word only because he grows poor, and a richer girl is ready to have him."

Mrs Jennings, Sense and Sensibility

The Miss Dashwoods were young, pretty, and unaffected. It was enough to secure his good opinion; for to be unaffected was all that a pretty girl could want to make her mind as captivating as her person.

Sense and Sensibility

FACT

Men and women could never meet without a chaperone in Jane Austen's time. Chaperones were usually family members and their role was to keep an eye on the behaviour of the couple and also listen to conversation to determine if they were compatible. Often the chaperone was the one who determined if the couple were to be married.

"One half of the world cannot understand the pleasures of the other."

Emma Woodhouse to her father, Emma

———————⊸∘OOo∘⊷———————

"One cannot know what a man really is by the end of a fortnight."

Mr Bennet, Pride and Prejudice

"One may be continually abusive without saying any thing just; but one cannot be always laughing at a man without now and then stumbling on something witty."

Elizabeth Bennet, *Pride and Prejudice*

THE TRIALS
AND DELIGHTS
OF MARRIAGE

Single women have a dreadful propensity for being poor — which is one very strong argument in favour of matrimony.

Letter to Fanny Knight, her niece

FACT

In 1802, when Jane and her sister had been visiting friends at Manydown House in Hampshire, Jane received a proposal (the only one she ever received) from Harris Bigg-Wither, a friend's younger brother and six years her junior. Jane initially accepted but then reconsidered overnight and withdrew her acceptance the next morning. She and Bigg-Wither managed to stay friends despite their near betrothal.

... having written so much on one side of the question, I shall now turn round and entreat you not to commit yourself farther, and not to think of accepting him unless you really do like him. Anything is to be preferred or endured rather than marrying without affection...

Letter to Fanny Knight, her niece

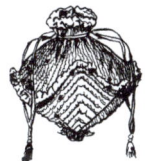

"Happiness in marriage is entirely a matter of chance."

Charlotte Lucas, Pride and Prejudice

Husbands and wives generally understand when opposition will be vain.

Persuasion

"... it is better to know as little as possible of the defects of the person with whom you are to pass your life."

Charlotte Lucas, *Pride and Prejudice*

"A woman is not to marry a man merely because she is asked, or because he is attached to her, and can write a tolerable letter."

Emma Woodhouse to Harriet Smith, *Emma*

TRIVIA

Finding a husband or wife went beyond falling in love with someone during Jane Austen's time. The match often had to be advantageous to the man, making it very hard for a woman who didn't have a family fortune to find herself a husband above a certain status. Indeed, a dowry could often make or break a relationship, but what was a dowry?

a) The permission of a woman's father to marry

b) A woman's acceptance of a proposal

c) Money, land or property that a woman's husband would receive once married

Jane wrote many lively and talkative characters, but one of them never says a word. Who?

a) Any of the servants

b) Georgiana Darcy, the sister of Mr Darcy in *Pride and Prejudice*

c) Miss Bates from *Emma*

"Oh! to be sure," cried Emma, "it is always incomprehensible to a man that a woman should ever refuse an offer of marriage. A man always imagines a woman to be ready for any body who asks her."

Emma Woodhouse to Mr Knightley, Emma

Lady Middleton resigned herself... contenting herself with merely giving her husband a gentle reprimand on the subject five or six times every day.

Sense and Sensibility

"I consider a country-dance as an emblem of marriage. Fidelity and complaisance are the principal duties of both; and those men who do not choose to dance or marry themselves, have no business with the partners or wives of their neighbours."

Henry Tilney to Catherine Morland,
Northanger Abbey

FACT

———————∞○○○∞———————

While marriage is a key theme in Jane Austen's novels and indeed in her life and the society she grew up in, there were many restrictions around marriage at that time. For example, the Hardwicke Marriage Act of 1754 ruled that a man and woman had to be at least 21 years old to get married. However, if a legal guardian gave their permission for an underage marriage, the happy couple could use a licence and go ahead with their nuptials.

———————∞○○○∞———————

"And such is your definition of matrimony and dancing. Taken in that light, certainly their resemblance is not striking; but I think I could place them in such a view. You will allow, that in both, man has the advantage of choice, woman only the power of refusal..."

Henry Tilney to Catherine Morland, Northanger Abbey

"Next to being married, a girl likes to be crossed a little in love now and then. It is something to think of, and it gives her a sort of distinction among her companions."

Mr Bennet to Elizabeth Bennet, Pride and Prejudice

"It is very hard to think that she might have been Mr Collins' wife by this time, had it not been for her own perverseness. He made her an offer in this very room, and she refused him. The consequence of it is, that Lady Lucas will have a daughter married before I have, and that the Longbourn estate is just as much entailed as ever."

Mrs Bennet on Elizabeth Bennet, *Pride and Prejudice*

FRIENDSHIP
AND FAMILY
MATTERS

"There is nothing I would not do for those who are really my friends. I have no notion of loving people by halves; it is not my nature."

Isabella Thorpe to Catherine Morland,
Northanger Abbey

FACT

Much of Jane Austen's writing focuses on family, so it may not be a surprise that the author came from a large family herself. The seventh of eight children, Jane had six brothers – James, George, Charles, Francis, Henry and Edward – and one sister, Cassandra.

The business of her life was to get her daughters married...

On Mrs Bennet, Pride and Prejudice

———————◦○○○◦———————

"Nobody, who has not been in the interior of a family, can say what the difficulties of any individual of that family may be."

Emma Woodhouse to Mr Knightley, Emma

"He has also brotherly pride, which, with some brotherly affection, makes him a very kind and careful guardian of his sister, and you will hear him generally cried up as the most attentive and best of brothers."

Mr Wickham on Mr Darcy, Pride and Prejudice

"Yes, I found myself, by insensible degrees, sincerely fond of her; and the happiest hours of my life were what I spent with her..."

Mr Willoughby to Elinor Dashwood,
Sense and Sensibility

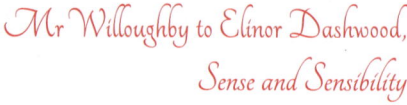

"Business, you know, may bring you money, but friendship hardly ever does."

Mr Knightley, Emma

Her own thoughts and reflections were habitually her best companions.

On Fanny Price, Mansfield Park

"But remember that the pain of parting from friends will be felt by everybody at times, whatever be their education or state."

Mrs Dashwood to Edward Ferrars, Sense and Sensibility

"My idea of good company... is the company of clever, well-informed people, who have a great deal of conversation..."

Anne Elliot, Persuasion

TRIVIA

Jane Austen's love of writing developed in her childhood, so much so that she wrote a book in her teens. It was full of adolescent angst and spelling mistakes, but was a clear blueprint for her future work. What was the name of the book Jane Austen wrote at the age of 14?

a) *Love, Life and Longeing*

b) *Familly and Foes*

c) *Love and Freindship*

At 21, Jane wrote her first full-length novel, *Elinor and Marianne*, which formed the basis of *Sense and Sensibility*. Her next book would come to be called *Pride and Prejudice*, but what was its original name?

a) *First Impressions*

b) *First Among Equals*

c) *First Refusal*

"Your mother will secure to you, in time, that independence you are so anxious for; it is her duty, and it will, it must ere long become her happiness to prevent your whole youth from being wasted in discontent."

Mrs Dashwood to Edward Ferrars, Sense and Sensibility

———————◦○○◦———————

"But people themselves alter so much, that there is something new to be observed in them forever."

Mr Darcy to Mrs Bennet, Pride and Prejudice

Friendship is certainly the
finest balm for the pangs
of disappointed love.

Northanger Abbey

FACT

Jane Austen wrote about strong female friendships throughout her novels. Most notable is the relationship between Elizabeth Bennet and Charlotte Lucas in *Pride and Prejudice*, but also unwavering is Elizabeth's fierce love and loyalty towards her sister Jane. These relationships are a powerful reflection of Jane Austen's own life as Jane's best friend was her older and only sister, Cassandra. In fact, their mother is quoted as saying: "If Cassandra were going to have her head cut off, Jane would insist on sharing the same fate."

It was very well known that no affection was ever supposed to exist between the children of any man by different marriages...

Sense and Sensibility

I do not want people to be very agreeable, as it saves me the trouble of liking them a great deal.

Letter to Cassandra

"For what do we live, but to
make sport for our neighbours,
and laugh at them in our turn?"

Mr Bennet, *Pride and Prejudice*

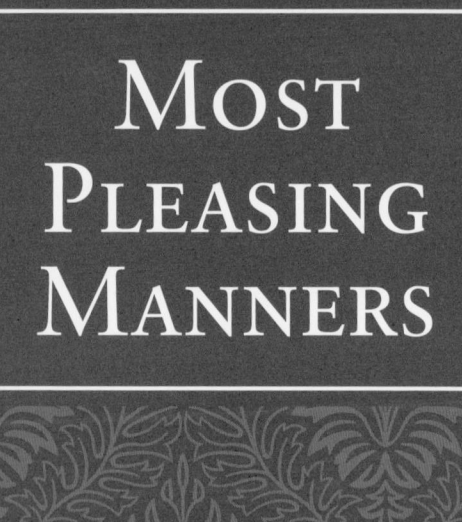

MOST
PLEASING
MANNERS

"In one respect, perhaps, Mr Elton's manners are superior to Mr Knightley's or Mr Weston's. They have more gentleness. They might be more safely held up as a pattern. There is an openness, a quickness, almost a bluntness in Mr Weston, which every body likes in him, because there is so much good-humour with it – but that would not do to be copied."

Emma Woodhouse to Harriet Smith, *Emma*

FACT

Nowadays it is generally accepted and encouraged for men to show their feelings. However, men in Jane Austen's time were always expected to be easy-going (or at least pretend to be) and it was never acceptable for a true gentleman to lose his temper in front of others. While women had to follow certain social rules, it was also understood that men had to control their facial expressions to never show their true feelings. They must also never be drawn into an argument in company, however frustrated they were.

"I do not know whether it ought to be so, but certainly silly things do cease to be silly if they are done by sensible people in an impudent way. Wickedness is always wickedness, but folly is not always folly."

Emma Woodhouse, Emma

———————∞○○○∞———————

"We have all a better guide in ourselves, if we would attend to it, than any other person can be."

Fanny Price to Henry Crawford, Mansfield Park

How quick come the reasons for approving what we like!

"Every time they met, it was more decided and remarkable. At his own ball he offended two or three young ladies, by not asking them to dance; and I spoke to him twice myself, without receiving an answer. Could there be finer symptoms? Is not general incivility the very essence of love?"

Elizabeth Bennet on Mr Bingley, *Pride and Prejudice*

Convinced as Elizabeth now was that Miss Bingley's dislike of her had originated in jealousy, she could not help feeling how very unwelcome her appearance at Pemberley must be to her, and was curious to know with how much civility on that lady's side the acquaintance would now be renewed.

Pride and Prejudice

TRIVIA

Of course, to participate in a dance during the Regency Era, you would have had lessons to learn the steps, and men would have needed to request a space on a lady's dance card. But, what other etiquette rule applied to men and women dancing together?

a) Women and men were only allowed to dance together three times at any one dance

b) Both must be wearing gloves

c) They must be a similar height

It is believed that Jane fell in love twice in her life, once with Tom Lefroy, who couldn't marry her because his family wanted someone wealthier, and later with a young clergyman she met in Sidmouth in Devon. They too failed to marry because…

a) He decided to marry someone else

b) Clergymen could not marry

c) He died before he could propose

Persuaded as Miss Bingley was that Darcy admired Elizabeth, this was not the best method of recommending herself; but angry people are not always wise; and in seeing him at last look somewhat nettled, she had all the success she expected.

Pride and Prejudice

Their conversation turned upon those subjects, of which the free discussion has generally much to do in perfecting a sudden intimacy between two young ladies: such as dress, balls, flirtations, and quizzes.

Northanger Abbey

"Mr Wickham is blessed with such happy manners as may ensure his making friends – whether he may be equally capable of retaining them, is less certain."

Mr Darcy to Elizabeth Bennet,
Pride and Prejudice

FACT

Many of Jane Austen's characters are competent in embroidery or knitting which is unsurprising as both of these skills were viewed as an attractive hobby to men and therefore were something to show off in public. However, more functional sewing, such as fixing torn dresses, was only to be done behind closed doors as it was not thought a polite thing to do in front of guests.

... I was as civil to them as their bad breath would allow me.

Letter to Cassandra

————⊶∞OΟOοc⊷————

"Good-humoured, unaffected girls, will not do for a man who has been used to sensible women. They are two distinct orders of being."

Edmund Bertram to Fanny Price, Mansfield Park

She was a benevolent, charitable, good woman, and capable of strong attachments, most correct in her conduct, strict in her notions of decorum, and with manners that were held a standard of good-breeding. She had a cultivated mind, and was, generally speaking, rational and consistent; but she had prejudices on the side of ancestry; she had a value for rank and consequence, which blinded her a little to the faults of those who possessed them.

On Lady Russell, Persuasion

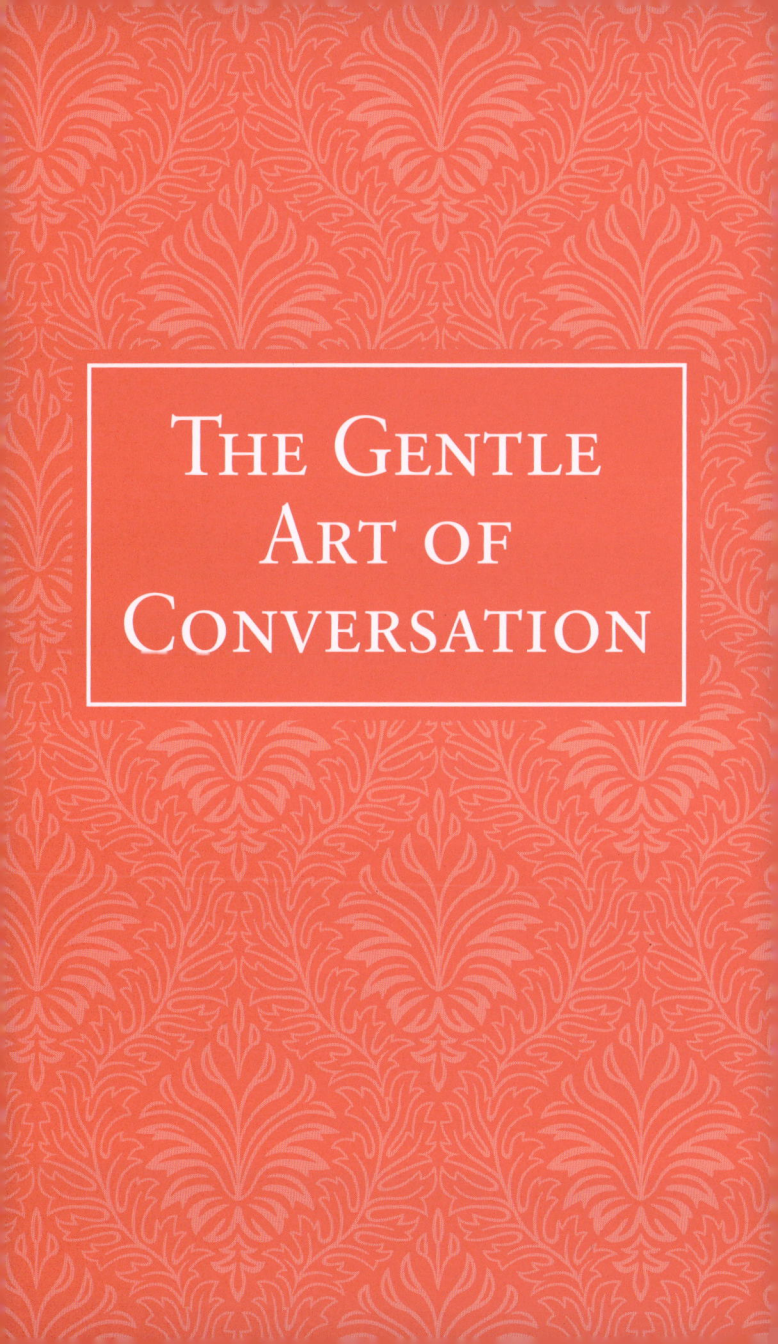

THE GENTLE
ART OF
CONVERSATION

... Mr Collins was to attend them, at the request of Mr Bennet, who was most anxious to get rid of him, and have his library to himself... but really talking to Mr Bennet, with little cessation, of his house and garden at Hunsford. Such doings discomposed Mr Bennet exceedingly. In his library he had been always sure of leisure and tranquillity; and though prepared, as he told Elizabeth, to meet with folly and conceit in every other room of the house, he was used to be free from them there...

Pride and Prejudice

FACT

─────────ꙮ─────────

While dinnertime rules today may be as simple as not using your phone at the table, during Jane Austen's era, things were a bit more complicated, especially around who you talked to and when.

Men were charged with entertaining those closest to them with engaging and humourous conversation. During the first course, conversation was directed to the left of the hostess. When the second course was served, the hostess reversed directions, signalling everyone else to turn and converse with whoever was on their right. This helped to reduce noise and was known as turning the table.

─────────ꙮ─────────

Their powers of conversation were considerable. They could describe an entertainment with accuracy, relate an anecdote with humour, and laugh at their acquaintance with spirit.

Pride and Prejudice

Mrs Allen was... never satisfied with the day unless she spent the chief of it by the side of Mrs Thorpe, in what they called conversation, but in which there was scarcely ever any exchange of opinion, and not often any resemblance of subject, for Mrs Thorpe talked chiefly of her children, and Mrs Allen of her gowns.

Northanger Abbey

He began to wish to know more of her, and as a step towards conversing with her himself, attended to her conversation with others.

On Mr Darcy, Pride and Prejudice

———————◦◦O◦◦———————

I have subdued him entirely by sentiment and serious conversation, and made him, I may venture to say, at least half in love with me, without the semblance of the most commonplace flirtation.

Lady Susan writing to Mrs Johnson, Lady Susan

———————◦◦O◦◦———————

She dearly loved her father, but he was no companion for her. He could not meet her in conversation, rational or playful.

Emma Woodhouse, Emma

TRIVIA

When Jane Austen was writing her novels, women were thought to be fair and fragile – well, the *right* sort of woman was anyway. With this in mind, what was a woman expected to do when confronted with foul language?

a) Faint

b) Unleash her own swear words

c) Cry

It has been voted the greatest moment in UK TV drama, Mr Darcy emerging from a lake in dripping breeches and a clinging white shirt in the 1995 adaptation of *Pride and Prejudice*. But who played Mr Darcy?

a) Daniel Craig

b) Colin Firth

c) Colin Farrell

Mrs Elton and Miss Bates are well contrasted; both are great talkers, but the conversation of the one is all vulgar egotism, while the other merely talks from inability to hold her tongue, and her chatter is always simple-minded and kind-hearted.

Emma

———————◦◯◦———————

"Your countenance perfectly informs me that you were in company last night with the person whom you think the most agreeable in the world, the person who interests you at this present time, more than all the rest of the world put together."

Mrs Smith to Anne Elliot, Persuasion

Luckily, the pleasures of friendship, of unreserved conversation, of similarity of taste and opinions will make good amends for orange wine.

Letter to Cassandra

FACT

Jane Austen loved to gossip, had a wicked sense of humour and was quick to poke fun at those around her. Sadly for Jane, scandal and gossip were not seen as appropriate topics of conversation for women. In fact, if anything to do with women's bodies, sexual relationships or scandalous topics were discussed, women were supposed to show utter shock and develop a pallor. Even laughing too much or too loudly was looked down upon.

Despite this, Jane and her sister, Cassandra, enjoyed sharing good gossip and filled their letters with all the titbits of information they gleaned and their "unladylike" thoughts.

"I always deserve the best treatment because I never put up with any other..."

Emma Woodhouse to Mr Knightley, Emma

"When you give me your opinion, I always know what is right. Your judgement is my rule of right."

Henry Crawford to Fanny Price, Mansfield Park

"What does Mr Darcy mean," said she to Charlotte, "by listening to my conversation with Colonel Forster?"

"That is a question which Mr Darcy only can answer."

"But if he does it any more I shall certainly let him know that I see what he is about. He has a very satirical eye, and if I do not begin by being impertinent myself, I shall soon grow afraid of him."

Elizabeth Bennet and Charlotte Lucas,
Pride and Prejudice

CLASS AND
FORTUNE

But there certainly are not so
many men of large fortune in
the world as there are pretty
women to deserve them.

Mansfield Park

FACT

Jane Austen was notoriously underpaid for her works and it is reported that she sold four of her books – basically her life's work – for a paltry £684 (which is around £67,000 today). She only earned £110 (about £10,800 today) for *Pride and Prejudice* despite it being one of her most successful novels and becoming an instant bestseller. Jane herself knew that she'd been underpaid – and often complained of it in her private correspondence.

"One cannot wonder that so very fine a young man, with family, fortune, everything in his favour, should think highly of himself."

Charlotte Lucas, *Pride and Prejudice*

———————◦○○○◦———————

"It is very difficult for the prosperous to be humble."

Frank Churchill writing to Mrs Weston, *Emma*

"What have wealth or grandeur to do with happiness?"

"Grandeur has but little," said Elinor, "but wealth has much to do with it."

Marianne Dashwood and Elinor Dashwood,
Sense and Sensibility

"The world is blinded by his fortune and consequence, or frightened by his high and imposing manners, and sees him only as he chooses to be seen."

Mr Wickham on Mr Darcy, Pride and Prejudice

"She is poor; she has sunk from the comforts she was born to; and, if she live to old age, must probably sink more. Her situation should secure your compassion."

Mr Knightley on Hetty Bates, Emma

TRIVIA

⸺∞○◯○∞⸺

Although Jane Austen may not have achieved the monetary success she deserved while she was alive, she ironically wound up connected to money. In 2017, she became the face of which UK bank note?

a) £5

b) £10

c) £20

⸺∞○◯○∞⸺

Jane's first four novels were published anonymously, as it was felt women should not write novels. Who was listed as the author?

a) A Lady

b) Currer Bell

c) Anonymous

"I mean to be too rich to lament or to feel anything of the sort. A large income is the best recipe for happiness I ever heard of."

Mary Crawford, *Mansfield Park*

Without thinking highly either of men or of matrimony, marriage had always been her object; it was the only honourable provision for well-educated young women of small fortune, and however uncertain of giving happiness, must be their pleasantest preservative from want.

On Charlotte Lucas, *Pride and Prejudice*

Harriet's parentage became known. She proved to be the daughter of a tradesman, rich enough to afford her the comfortable maintenance which had ever been hers, and decent enough to have always wished for concealment – Such was the blood of gentility which Emma had formerly been so ready to vouch for! – It was likely to be as untainted, perhaps, as the blood of many a gentleman: but what a connexion had she been preparing for Mr Knightley – or for the Churchills – or even for Mr Elton! – The stain of illegitimacy, unbleached by nobility or wealth, would have been a stain indeed.

Emma

FACT

The wealthiest men in Jane Austen's novels may have very different personalities but they are all the same in one significant way: none has a job and their incomes came, as was common, from inherited wealth and land. Mr Rushworth in *Mansfield Park* is the richest of all characters with an income of £12,000 a year (about £1,180,900 today). Along with his brooding good looks, Mr Darcy of *Pride and Prejudice* has an equally attractive annual income of £10,000 (about £984,000 today) and Henry Crawford from *Mansfield Park* boasts an income of £4,000 (about £394,000 today).

It is a truth universally acknowledged, that a single man in possession of a good fortune, must be in want of a wife.

Pride and Prejudice

———————————oOOoc———————————

"Yes; it is in two points offensive to me; I have two strong grounds of objection to it. First, as a means of bringing persons of obscure birth into undue distinction, and raising men to honours which their fathers and grandfathers never dreamt of; and secondly, as it cuts up a man's youth and vigour most horribly."

Sir Walter Elliot on the Navy, Persuasion

"To walk three miles, or four miles, or five miles, or whatever it is, above her ankles in dirt, and alone, quite alone! What could she mean by it? It seems to me to show an abominable sort of conceited independence, a most country-town indifference to decorum."

Caroline Bingley on Elizabeth Bennet,
Pride and Prejudice

Quick Wit,
Gossip and
Wicked Insults

I suppose you know all about the Wars between him and the Duke of York who was of the right side; if you do not, you had better read some other History, for I shall not be very diffuse in this, meaning by it only to vent my spleen against, and shew my Hatred to all those people whose parties or principles do not suit with mine, and not to give information. This King married Margaret of Anjou, a woman whose distresses and misfortunes were so great as almost to make me who hate her, pity her.

The History of England... By a Partial, Prejudiced, & Ignorant Historian

FACT

—————————∞○○○∝—————————

Jane's best friend and favourite person to gossip with was her sister Cassandra. Hundreds of letters passed between the two documenting Jane's thoughts on love, life, society and their mutual family and friends. While a few of the letters remain, Cassandra (who was fiercely protective of Jane) burned hundreds of Jane's letters after she died in order to keep them secret and protect friends and family members from finding out how they had been mocked by the witty writer.

—————————∞○○○∝—————————

The whole of Lucy's behaviour in the affair, and the prosperity which crowned it, therefore, may be held forth as a most encouraging instance of what an earnest, an unceasing attention to self-interest, however its progress may be apparently obstructed, will do in securing every advantage of fortune, with no other sacrifice than that of time and conscience.

Sense and Sensibility

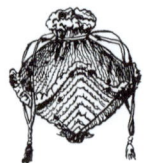

"And I have no doubt that he will thrive, and be a very rich man in time – and his being illiterate and coarse need not disturb us."

Emma Woodhouse on Robert Weston, Emma

"Miss Morland, no one can think more highly of the understanding of women than I do. In my opinion, nature has given them so much that they never find it necessary to use more than half."

Henry Tilney, Northanger Abbey

———————∞OOO∞———————

"I take no leave of you, Miss Bennet. I send no compliments to your mother. You deserve no such attention. I am most seriously displeased."

Lady Catherine, Pride & Prejudice

———————∞OOO∞———————

"I shall not pay them any such compliment, I assure you. I have no notion of treating men with such respect. That is the way to spoil them."

Isabella Thorpe to Catherine Morland,
Northanger Abbey

TRIVIA

———————◦○○○◦———————

Jane Austen was known for her acerbic wit and intelligence, so in which of her novels does she parody the gothic novels that were popular at the time for their sensational tales of mystery and horror?

a) *Emma*

b) *Northanger Abbey*

c) *Mansfield Park*

———————◦○○○◦———————

And which of her novels is a bestseller, with over 20 million copies sold?

a) *Sense and Sensibility*

b) *Mansfield Park*

c) *Pride and Prejudice*

... she was very plain and her name was Bridget... Nothing therefore could be expected from her... She was nothing more than a mere good-tempered, civil and obliging young woman; as such we could scarcely dislike here [sic] – she was only an Object of Contempt.

Love and Freindship

———————◦○○○◦———————

She was of course only too good for him; but as nobody minds having what is too good for them, he was very steadily earnest in the pursuit of the blessing...

On Edmund Bertram, Mansfield Park

"You are mistaken, Mr Darcy, if you suppose that the mode of your declaration affected me in any other way, than as it spared the concern which I might have felt in refusing you, had you behaved in a more gentlemanlike manner."

Elizabeth Bennet, *Pride and Prejudice*

FACT

One of the reasons for Jane Austen's enduring appeal is that her work continues to be relevant to readers across all ages and eras. This is especially clear in Jane's teenage writings which could easily have referenced today's adolescents. In her early works, characters behaved badly in a timeless way – getting involved with each other's boyfriends, drinking, fighting and stealing money.

Mrs Hall, of Sherborne, was brought to bed yesterday of a dead child, some weeks before she expected, owing to a fright. I suppose she happened unawares to look at her husband.

Letter to Cassandra

Mrs Allen was one of that numerous class of females, whose society can raise no other emotion than surprise at there being any men in the world who could like them well enough to marry them. She had neither beauty, genius, accomplishment, nor manner.

Northanger Abbey

Where people wish to attach, they should always be ignorant. To come with a well-informed mind is to come with an inability of administering to the vanity of others, which a sensible person would always wish to avoid. A woman especially, if she have the misfortune of knowing anything, should conceal it as well as she can.

Northanger Abbey

HIGH
SOCIETY

It would be mortifying to the feelings of many ladies, could they be made to understand how little the heart of man is affected by what is costly or new in their attire; how little it is biased by the texture of their muslin, and how unsusceptible of peculiar tenderness towards the spotted, the sprigged, the mull, or the jackonet. Woman is fine for her own satisfaction alone. No man will admire her the more, no woman will like her the better for it. Neatness and fashion are enough for the former, and a something of shabbiness or impropriety will be most endearing to the latter.

Northanger Abbey

FACT

While Jane and her family were not of the highest society they were still on the fringes, which meant Jane was very aware of what was happening in fashionable society. In her mid-twenties she moved to the town of Bath, a popular place to live thanks to its hot springs, which were used as a health resort for those who had the funds. It's no surprise that the author also chose to base two of her novels, *Northanger Abbey* and *Persuasion*, in Bath where she could observe and be inspired by the many members of society all around her.

"Nothing is more deceitful... than the appearance of humility. It is often only carelessness of opinion, and sometimes an indirect boast."

Mr Darcy, Pride and Prejudice

"I never in my life saw a man more intent on being agreeable than Mr Elton. It is downright labour to him where ladies are concerned. With men he can be rational and unaffected, but when he has ladies to please, every feature works."

Mr Knightley, Emma

Nothing could be more delightful! To be fond of dancing was a certain step towards falling in love; and very lively hopes of Mr Bingley's heart were entertained.

Pride and Prejudice

We are to have a tiny party here tonight; I hate tiny parties – they force one into constant exertion.

Letter to Cassandra

"Nothing ever fatigues me but doing what I do not like."

Mary Crawford, Mansfield Park

TRIVIA

Moving in the correct social circles was very important in the world of Jane Austen and the Regency Era. The word *ton* is often used to describe society and was taken from the French *le bon ton* but what does it actually refer to?

a) The town where society people live

b) Fashionable society

c) Something very heavy

As well as direct film adaptations of her work, there have been looser versions. Which of the following is not based on a Jane Austen novel?

a) *Clueless*

b) *Bridget Jones' Diary*

c) *Mean Girls*

"Selfishness must always be forgiven, you know, because there is no hope of a cure."

Mary Crawford to Fanny Price, Mansfield Park

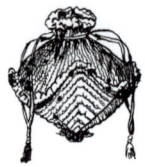

"Going in dismal weather, to return probably in worse; – four horses and four servants taken out for nothing but to convey five idle, shivering creatures into colder rooms and worse company than they might have had at home."

Mr Knightley, Emma

The melancholy part was to see so many dozen young women standing by without partners, and each of them with two ugly naked shoulders.

Letter to Cassandra

FACT

With the absence of streaming services, social media or any of the other quick-fix forms of entertainment that we enjoy today, wealthy households from the Regency Era often put on their own music events. These almost always featured family members who could sing or play an instrument, which is one of the reasons why women were encouraged and even expected to learn music.

"But really, ma'am, I think it would be very hard upon younger sisters, that they should not have their share of society and amusement, because the elder may not have the means or inclination to marry early."

Elizabeth Bennet to Lady Catherine, Pride and Prejudice

━━━━━◦○○○◦━━━━━

Vanity was the beginning and the end of Sir Walter Elliot's character; vanity of person and of situation. He had been remarkably handsome in his youth; and, at fifty-four, was still a very fine man. Few women could think more of their personal appearance than he did, nor could the valet of any new made lord be more delighted with the place he held in society. He considered the blessing of beauty as inferior only to the blessing of a baronetcy; and the Sir Walter Elliot, who united these gifts, was the constant object of his warmest respect and devotion.

Persuasion

"If he knew them better,
he would value their society
as it deserves; for they
are in fact exactly the sort
of people he would like."

Edmund Bertram to Fanny Price,
Mansfield Park

ONE MUST BE HIGHLY ACCOMPLISHED

He knew her to be clever, to have a quick apprehension as well as good sense, and a fondness for reading, which, properly directed, must be an education in itself.

Edmund Bertram on Fanny Price,
Mansfield Park

FACT

————————∞◦○○◦∞————————

When she wasn't working on her latest novel, Jane spent much of her spare time pursuing her other love – music. It was reported that she played the piano daily and sang for family and close friends. Jane also collected sheet music to support her hobby and she often woke up early to have some time to play the piano by herself before the rest of her family were up. She declared it helpful for her mental focus and the rhythm of her music carried effortlessly through to her beautiful writing. It's unsurprising that music and performance feature heavily in much of her work.

————————∞◦○○◦∞————————

"... they are much to be pitied who have not been taught to feel, in some degree, as you do; who have not, at least, been given a taste for Nature in early life. They lose a great deal."

Edmund Bertram to Fanny Price, Mansfield Park

"We are speaking of music, Madam," said he, when no longer able to avoid a reply.

"Of music! Then pray speak aloud. It is of all subjects my delight. I must have my share in the conversation, if you are speaking of music. There are few people in England, I suppose, who have more true enjoyment of music than myself, or a better natural taste. If I had ever learnt, I should have been a great proficient."

Colonel Fitzwilliam and Lady Catherine,
Pride and Prejudice

"Give a girl an education, and introduce her properly into the world, and ten to one but she has the means of settling well, without farther expense to anybody."

Mrs Norris, Mansfield Park

———∞OOO∞———

She was not much deceived as to her own skill either as an artist or a musician, but she was not unwilling to have others deceived, or sorry to know her reputation for accomplishment often higher than it deserved.

On Emma Woodhouse, Emma

———∞OOO∞———

"No governess! How was that possible? Five daughters brought up at home without a governess! I never heard of such a thing. Your mother must have been quite a slave to your education."

Lady Catherine to Elizabeth Bennet, Pride and Prejudice

TRIVIA

———————◦○◯○◦———————

In *Pride and Prejudice*, Mr Darcy agrees with Caroline Bingley about what sorts of knowledge an accomplished woman should possess ranging from modern languages to music to being well read. With this in mind, how many accomplished women does Mr Darcy claim to know?

a) None

b) At least 20

c) No more than half a dozen

———————◦○◯○◦———————

Jane Austen died in 1817. She is buried in a place visited by Cassandra and Ben in the 2011 novel, *The Time Baroness* by Georgina Young-Ellis. Where is it?

a) Westminster Cathedral

b) Winchester Cathedral

c) Highgate Cemetery

There was a numerous family; but the only two grown up, excepting Charles, were Henrietta and Louisa, young ladies of nineteen and twenty, who had brought from school at Exeter all the usual stock of accomplishments, and were now like thousands of other young ladies, living to be fashionable, happy, and merry.

Persuasion

———————⊷⧫◯◯◯⧫⊶———————

"The person, be it gentleman or lady, who has not pleasure in a good novel, must be intolerably stupid."

Henry Tilney, Northanger Abbey

"You, Miss Woodhouse, I well know, play delightfully. I assure you it has been the greatest satisfaction, comfort, and delight to me, to hear what a musical society I am got into. I absolutely cannot do without music. It is a necessary of life to me; and having always been used to a very musical society, both at Maple Grove and in Bath, it would have been a most serious sacrifice."

Mrs Elton to Emma Woodhouse, Emma

FACT

———⊃○○○⊂———

Jane Austen is heralded as one of the most talented and esteemed novelists of all time. But her formal education ended abruptly at the age of 11, when she was forced to leave Abbey Girls' School in Reading. She had been taught the basics in writing and spelling, along with other topics and went on to read extensively from her father's library, educating herself throughout her teenage years.

———⊃○○○⊂———

Mr Collins was not a sensible man, and the deficiency of nature had been but little assisted by education or society; the greatest part of his life having been spent under the guidance of an illiterate and miserly father; and though he belonged to one of the universities, he had merely kept the necessary terms, without forming at it any useful acquaintance.

Pride and Prejudice

"But it is his way. One man's style must not be the rule of another's."

Mr Knightley, Emma

"How pleasant it is to spend an evening in this way! I declare after all there is no enjoyment like reading! How much sooner one tires of anything than of a book! When I have a house of my own, I shall be miserable if I have not an excellent library."

Caroline Bingley, *Pride and Prejudice*

ANSWERS

Sir David Attenborough: A Treasure Trove

Debbi Marco

Hardback

ISBN: 978-1-83799-647-6

This keepsake is an ode to our most beloved broadcaster, biologist and environmentalist, packed to the brim with facts, trivia questions and a selection of his most insightful and inspiring quotes. Celebrate the incredible richness of the natural world around us and discover a hopeful outlook for the future, through Sir Attenborough's eyes.

Quotable Austen: Memorable Quotes from Our Favourite Writer

Max Morris

Hardback

ISBN: 978-1-83799-643-8

With over 140 quotes from Jane Austen's completed novels – *Sense and Sensibility*, *Pride and Prejudice*, *Mansfield Park*, *Emma*, *Northanger Abbey* and *Persuasion* – this book is the perfect opportunity for readers to immerse themselves in the refinement of the Regency Era.

IMAGE CREDITS

Have you enjoyed this book? If so, find us on Facebook at **Summersdale Publishers**, on Twitter/X at **@Summersdale** and on Instagram and TikTok at **@summersdalebooks** and get in touch. We'd love to hear from you!

www.summersdale.com